A Perfect Place for a Perfect Reunion

YANICK LOUIS

No part of this publication may be reproduced, stored in a retrieval system or transmitted in any form or by any means, electronic, mechanical, photocopying, recording, or otherwise, without express written permission of the author.

A Perfect Place for A Perfect Reunion
A Promise From the Garden

Yanick Louis
ylouis20@aol.com

©Copyright 2020 All rights reserved

ISBN 978-1-949027-70-9

Published by:
Destined To Publish | www.DestinedToPublish.com
Flossmoor, Illinois • 773-783-2981

Dedication

Thanks Mom!

Growing up,
Christmas was always special
because of you.

It was a
Perfect Place
for a reunion!

But no one
knew it!

It was
Christmas Eve.
We were so excited!
The living room was bright, lit
up with the Christmas tree.

Presents, presents everywhere!
We could not wait
to open them all on
Christmas Day!

Every year,
Dad would read us the
Christmas Story.
We loved it!

Sleepy-eyed
and yawning,
we listened eagerly.

And, suddenly,
I was there!
It was like a dream,
in another world.

All the way back at the
beginning.

Whoa!

I felt like I had
special eyes to see!
And I could see!

Jesus together with God,
creating the world. Everything
in the world. The moon.
The stars. All the animals.

Wow! Amazing!

Then God did
something super special!

He created
the perfect man.
One that looked
just like Him.

He named him
Adam,
the father of all humankind:
you, me, and
everyone on Earth.

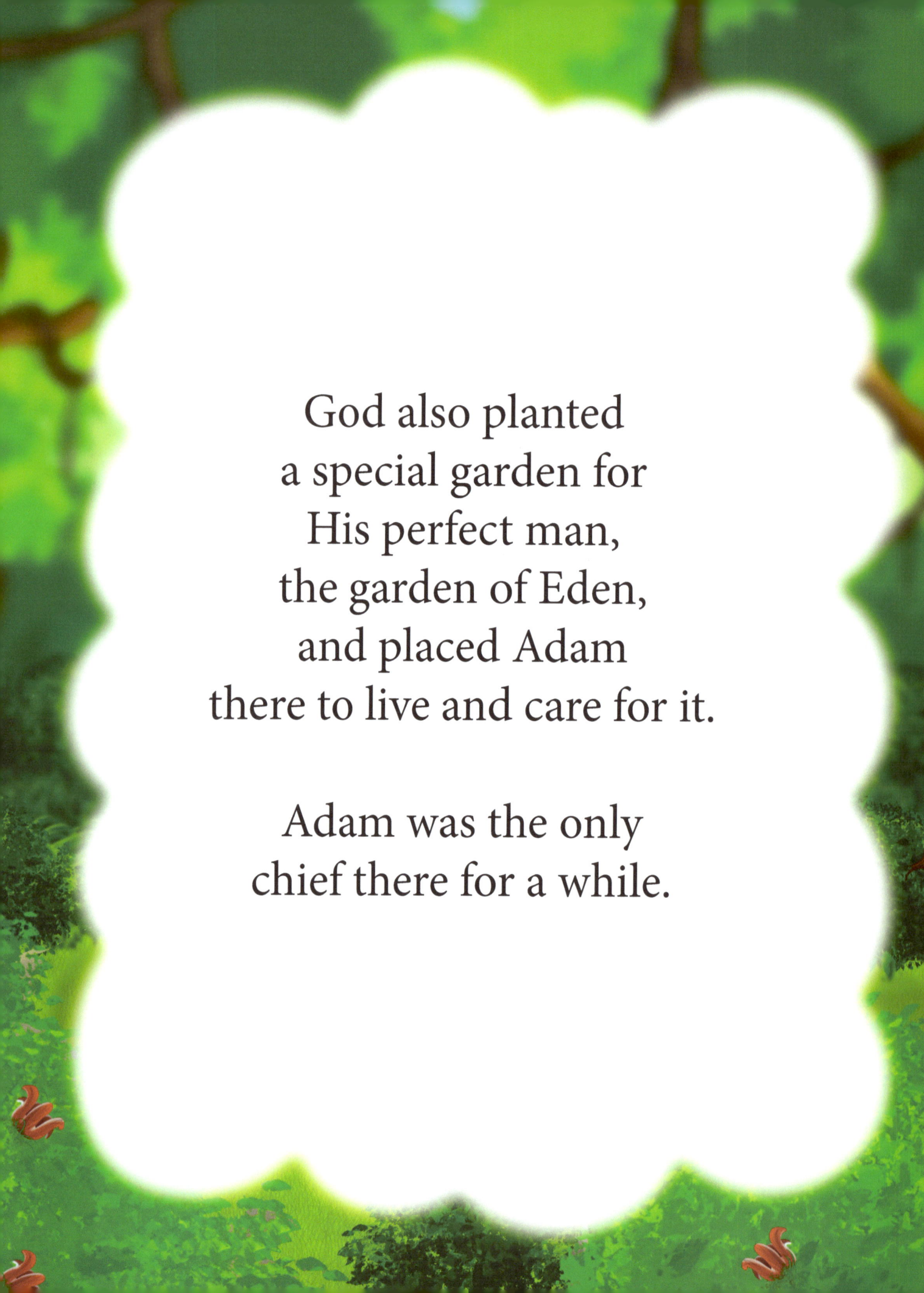

God also planted
a special garden for
His perfect man,
the garden of Eden,
and placed Adam
there to live and care for it.

Adam was the only
chief there for a while.

But later,
God created Adam's wife.

Her name was
Eve.

But, sadly,
the man did not stay perfect,
like God created him.

He and his wife ate the fruit in
the garden God had told him
not to eat.

They spoiled everything.

From that time on,
God and His people
became separated.
And His perfect man had to
leave the garden.

But God did not want
to stay separated
from His people.

So, right there,
in the garden of Eden,
the plan for this beautiful,
awesome reunion began.

Today, we call it

Christmas,

A reunion between God
and His people
through the birth of
His Son, Jesus.

The preparation for this awesome reunion took a very long time.

But, along the way, God sent His people reminders through His trusted messengers, the prophets.

God wanted them to always keep watching for Jesus' soon coming. Everything had to be perfect for Jesus to be born on Earth.

First, He sent His prophet Isaiah
to tell His people,
*"A virgin will give birth
to a Son."*

One of His names will be
Immanuel,
which means,
"God with us."

God and His people would be
together again,
like before, in the garden.

Later,
the prophet Micah
came.

He told them,
*"The Savior will be born
in Bethlehem."*

And when it was almost time for the reunion, God sent his special angel Gabriel to the small town of Galilee to speak to a young woman named *Mary.* She was engaged to be married to a man named *Joseph.*

At first, Mary was puzzled and afraid when she saw the angel.

But the angel said to her, *"Don't be afraid, Mary. God is very pleased with you. And because of that, He has chosen you to do something special. You will give birth to a Son. He will be called the Son of God. You will name Him Jesus."*

Mary gladly agreed, saying, *"I am happy to do what God wants."*

But Joseph was not sure.
So an angel
also appeared to him in a
dream and said to him,
*"Joseph, don't be afraid to take
Mary as your wife.
The Baby who will be born is
from God, the Holy Spirit."*

Then, just like Mary,
Joseph was happy and agreed.
And soon after they received
this awesome news, the Baby
began to grow in Mary's belly.

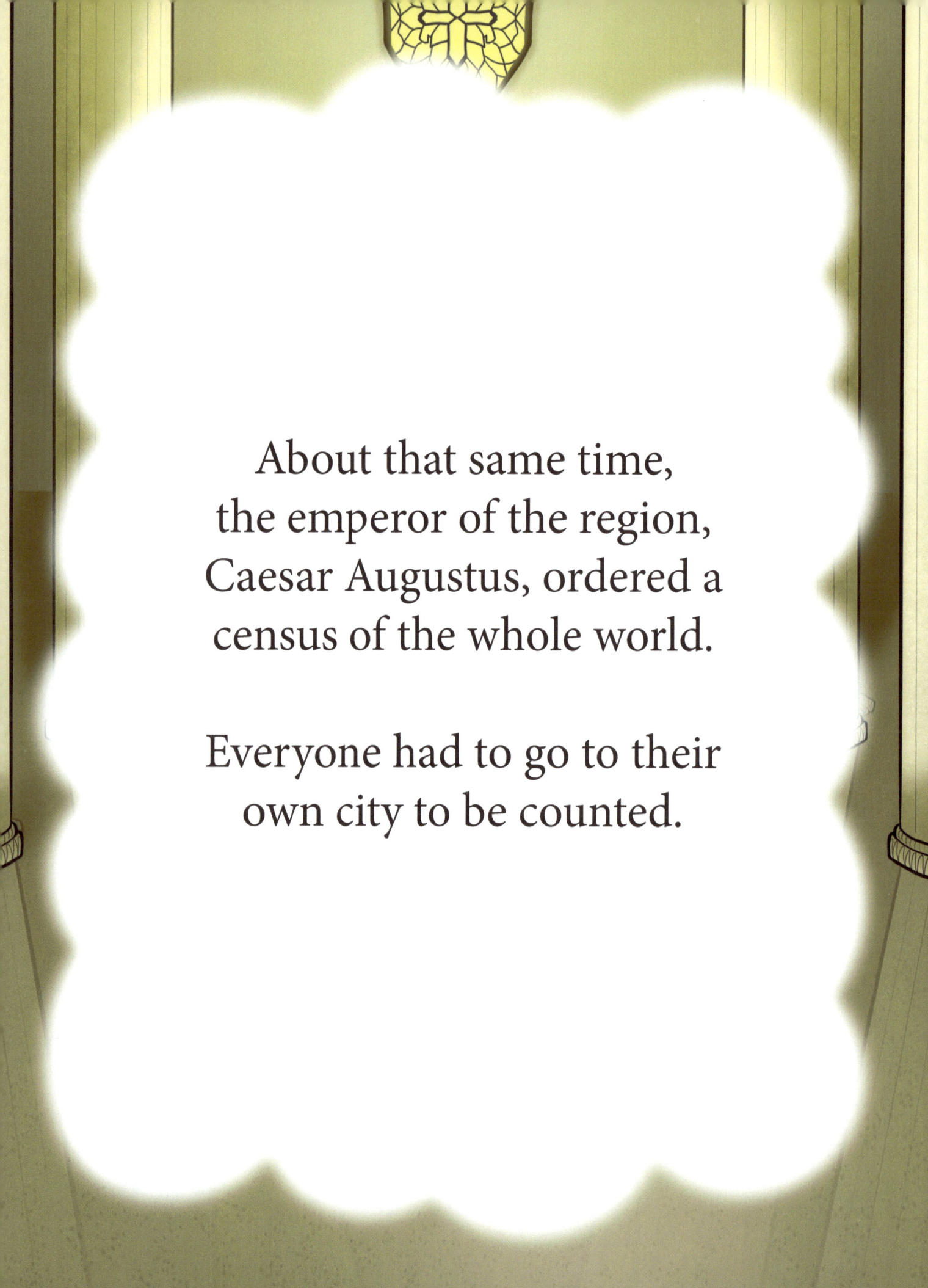

About that same time,
the emperor of the region,
Caesar Augustus, ordered a
census of the whole world.

Everyone had to go to their
own city to be counted.

Now everyone was making
their way to their own city.

Mary, Joseph, and
the soon to be born
Babe made the trip, too.

The crowd grew bigger
and bigger.
The town bursting with people.

All the innkeepers at their
doors, saying,
"No room in the inn,"
"No room in the inn."

Finally, an offer of a barn.
Yes! There, they rested.

That same night, Mary gave birth to her Firstborn Son.

She wrapped Him in swaddling clothes and laid Him in a manger.

There were shepherds in nearby fields, watching over their sheep. Suddenly an angel appeared before them, with bright and shining lights all around them.

The shepherds were so scared. But the angel told them, *"Don't be afraid. I bring you good news of great joy that will be for all people. Today, in the city of David, a Savior is born who is Christ the Lord. This will be a sign to you: you will find a Babe wrapped in swaddling clothes, lying in a manger."*

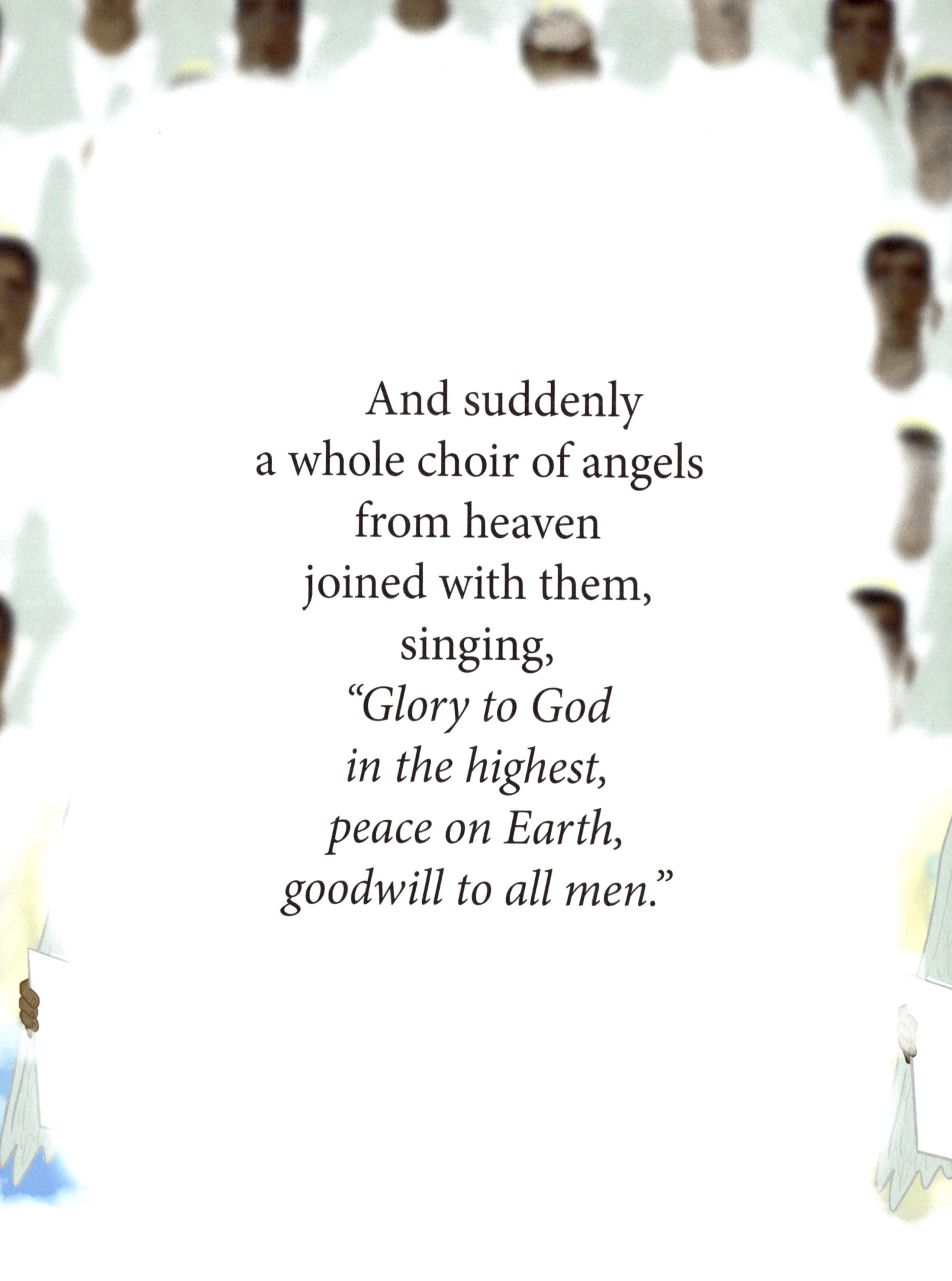

And suddenly
a whole choir of angels
from heaven
joined with them,
singing,
"*Glory to God
in the highest,
peace on Earth,
goodwill to all men.*"

When the angels left,
the shepherds
excitedly rushed to
Bethlehem
to see this great thing.

And when they came,
they found Mary, Joseph,
and the Babe,
just like the angel had said.

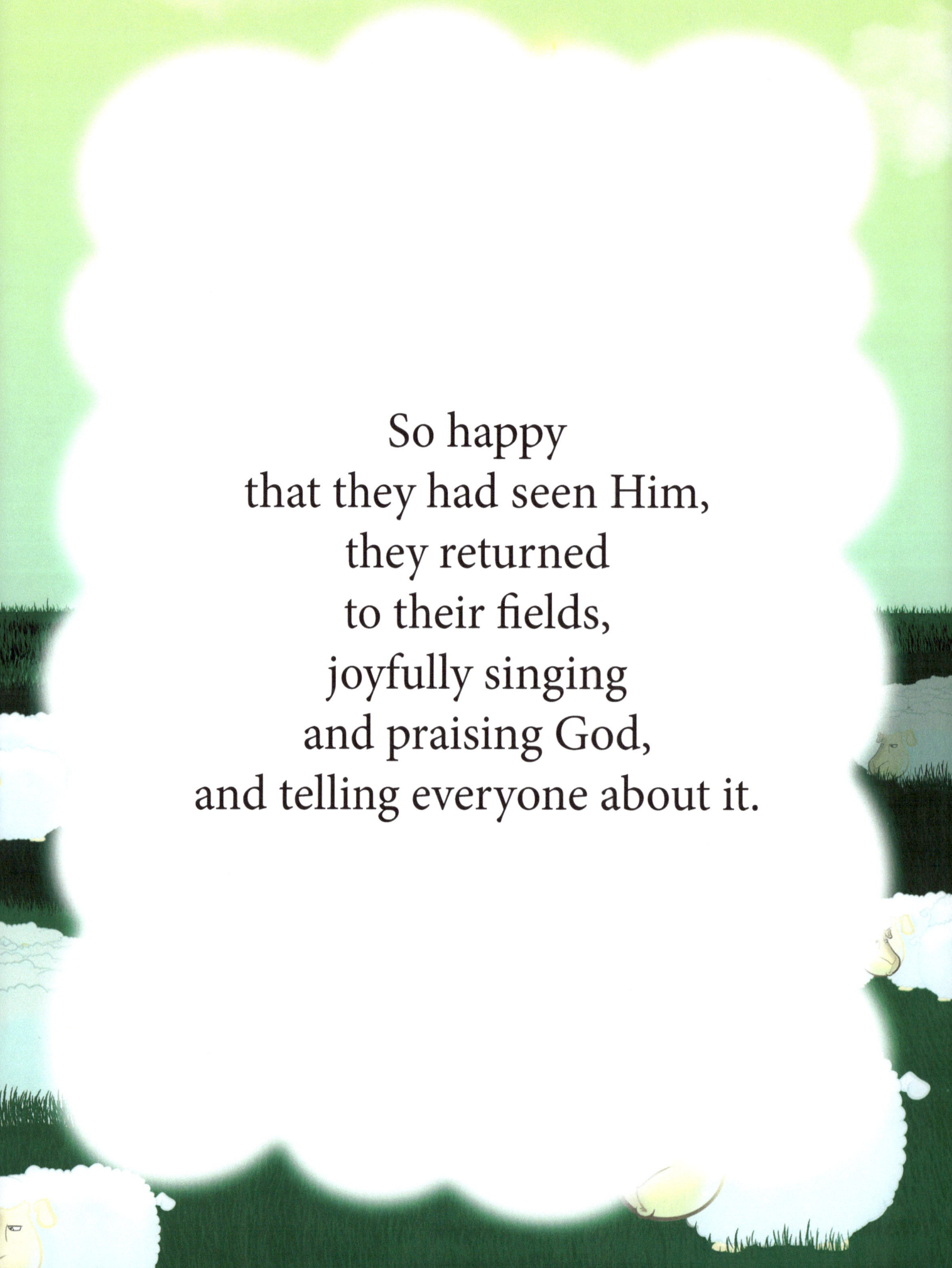

So happy
that they had seen Him,
they returned
to their fields,
joyfully singing
and praising God,
and telling everyone about it.

Later, after Jesus's birth,
wise men from a faraway land
in the East came, guided by a
special star in the sky.

They arrived in Jerusalem,
asking,
*"Where is the king of the Jews
who was born?
For we have seen His star."*

"Bethlehem,"
the people answered.
So, the men departed and
followed the star.

When they arrived,
the star stopped right above
where Jesus was.
There, the wise men found Him
with his mother Mary.

And just like the shepherds,
they were happy.
They fell to their knees and
worshipped Him,
opening their treasures and
giving Him lots of gifts:
gold, frankincense,
and myrrh.

Not everyone
came together at once.
Those close by, like the
shepherds, came quickly.
And those far away, like the
wise men, took a little longer.

It was still
a perfect reunion . . .
in a barn, of all places!
For all, the shepherds,
the wise men,
and everyone were happy
and full of joy
when they saw Him.

It was the first
Christmas.

Suddenly,
I heard a gentle whisper
in my ear.

*"Wake up, honey.
It's Christmas Day!"*

From that first Christmas on,
every year
the invitation goes out.
A family reunion.
You all come!
But don't wait until Christmas!
Come any day,
any time.
To the best reunion ever!
God. Jesus. People.
Together again!

About the Author

Yanick Louis worked for years as a pediatric nurse. She loves children.

A Perfect Place for a Perfect Reunion, her debut book was born out of her warmest childhood memories with her family.

She's a mom, and now a proud grandma to two precious little girls. Originally from Haiti, Yanick and her family now reside in Florida.

www.ingramcontent.com/pod-product-compliance
Lightning Source LLC
Chambersburg PA
CBHW040032110426
42738CB00048B/52